The RED MAMMOTH

Written by **Sanjeeb & Sasmita Patel**

Illustrated by **Nadia Ilchuk**

Author: Sanjeeb & Sasmita Patel • Illustrator: Nadia Ilchuk
Graphic Design & Layout by Nicole Lavoie, JustSayingDezigns.com

sanjeebpatel@gmail.com • sasmita.patel@gmail.com
https://www.facebook.com/TheRedMammoth
First Printing October 2019

My Papa,

I still remember those days when I was a little baby and would ask you to tell bedtime stories. It would normally go like this:

Me: Papa! Story, story... I want a story, I want a story.

Papa: Ok... Ok... Hmm... Once upon a time there was big jungle, Really big big jungle with huge trees and lots of animals. Tigers... Lions... Giraffes...

Me: Then????

Papa: Hmm... Zebras... Monkeys... Donkeys... Bears... ummm...

(The list would go on and on until you couldn't remember any more animal names)

...and with them there was a Red Elephant *(pause)*

Me: Then????

Papa: There was a Blue Elephant... *(pause)*

Me: Then????

Papa: There was a Yellow Elephant... *(pause)*

Me: Then????

Papa: There was a Black Elephant... *(pause)*

Me: Then????

...And it goes on and on like this until I fall asleep cuddling you.

There was no story in it, but it was one of my favorite stories which I still remember. The way you described everything made me think I was in the jungle and living the story. That also generated curiosity in me and I started imagining jungles, trees, nature, animals, and different kinds of Elephants. Even Elephants with different patterns, black & white like a Zebra. Can you believe it? I lost my father back in 2000 and today I, along with my wife Sasmita, have written our first children's book dedicated to my Papa, late Gopal Chandra Patel.

Thanks Papa. Love you sooooooo much!

Sanjeeb

A long time ago, there was a family
that lived in a small hut in the jungle.

By growing up in the jungle, the little girl,
Mia became friends with the jungle animals.

One day, when Papa was out searching for firewood,
a tiger came into the hut looking for food.

Mama fought with
the tiger to keep Mia safe.

6

When Papa returned to the hut,
he found little Mia crying.

Ever since that day,
Papa had a hatred
for wild animals.

He raised Mia by himself and would
tell her bedtime stories that were filled
with hatred toward animals.

One night, Mia saw a red Mammoth in her dream
and asked Papa to get her one.

Papa told Mia that Mammoths are extinct
and he would not be able to get one.

That didn't stop Mia from
asking for one every day.

11

With Papa being a hunter, Mia would see
the animals and become very sad.

One day, when Papa was aiming for an animal,
that looked a lot like a baby mammoth, Mia screamed.

The scream scared the
animal and it ran away.
Mia had saved its life.

As time passed, summer arrived and the jungle was dry.
Papa was out hunting when a fire broke out.

16

He was surrounded by flames
and could not escape.

Back at the hut, Mia was alone and eagerly waiting for Papa to return.
18

She waited and waited, but Papa did not show up.

As the sun began to set, Mia got really scared
and prayed for her Papa's safe return.

As night fell on the jungle,
Mia was able to see red flames in the distance.

Then she heard noises coming
from outside the hut.

Mia ran outside and could see a
giant figure in the distance.

As the figure got closer
Mia was able to see it was a
Mammoth with Papa on its back.

Mia could not believe her eyes.
It was a red Mammoth!

When the red Mammoth reached the hut,
Papa jumped down off its back.

Mia was so happy.

The red Mammoth slowly headed back into the jungle
where the baby mammoth was waiting.

Papa never forgot how the Mammoth
had saved his life that night.

He had a new found respect
and love for all animals.

Papa and Mia continued to share the jungle
with the animals and gave each other the space
they needed to live in harmony.

Woolly Mammoths were closely related to today's Asian elephants. Extinct about 4,000 years ago when the last ice age ended. While most did indeed die out 10,000 years ago, one tiny population endured on isolated Wrangel Island until 1650 BCE. The last woolly mammoths were still alive while the Great Pyramid was being built.

Size: 9-14 feet at the shoulder.

Weight: 6-10 tons. Newborns weighed approximately 90kg at birth.

Hair: A fur coat in 2 layers, good for cold weather. The thick, long, shaggy outer-coat (which is why they are called "woolly") and a fine, short undercoat. They had about 4 inches of pure fat for insulation underneath their skin.

Teeth & Tusks: Special teeth with ridges, grew 5 or 6 sets in their life, had no enamel, added a growth ring every year. Once a tooth is worn down from too much grinding, a new tooth grows behind it. The new tooth slowly moves forward and pushes the old one out. Tusks are teeth that extend from the mammoth's mouth. The tusks of the woolly mammoth were often quite dramatically curved. Mammoth's tusk can range from 10-15 foot in length. The tusks help researchers identify the age. Just like a tree, a cross section of a tusk reveals growth rings that reveal the Mammoth's age. Mammoth's tusk would grow more during favorable conditions. Tusk has line for each year and a line for the weeks and days in between. It was used in a variety of tasks - brushing off snow from the ground while searching for food, as a show of strength to deter predators and fight one another for territory and mating.

Diet: Mammoths were herbivores, grazers. They ate leaves, grasses, sedges, bushes, willow, and fir. They probably ate about 700 pounds of grass and leaves each day.

Life Span: Between 60 and 80 years.

Woolly Mammoth Facts

Why Mammoth's ears were small?

Mammoths had smaller ears because they lived in colder climates. They needed to conserve as much heat as possible. Smaller ears minimized frostbite and heat loss. Woolly Mammoth's ears only reached about 30 cm.

What did baby Mammoth eat?

Young mammoths, not being able to chew the grass properly, consumed the feces of adults. The dung used to give their digestive system the correct bacteria.

Why did humans kill Woolly Mammoths?

Humans killed Woolly Mammoths for several reasons. They ate the meat, but they also made art, homes and tools out of the bones and tusks. Mammoth bones were even used in burials.

Why did the Woolly Mammoth become extinct?

A definitive reason for why they became extinct is not available; however, most scientists believe climate change caused its demise. Some think humans killed last few Mammoths causing their extinction where as some think the demise of the woolly mammoth may have been caused by the sudden impact of a meteorite or comet hitting the Earth.

Woolly Mammoth Facts

Who are "Lyuba" and "Khroma"?

Several complete woolly mammoth carcasses have been discovered preserved in the permafrost of Siberia. One of them is a baby woolly mammoth that had been washed out from the permafrost along the Yuribei River was found in 2007. Frozen for more than 40,000 years, she was in nearly perfect shape--skin and internal organs intact, taste buds on her tongue, last meal in her stomach. Almost four feet long and weighing about 50 Kg, she even still had some hair and toenails. She was nicknames "Lyuba". A specimen like Lyuba, with so much soft tissue intact, is extremely rare. Another skeleton of a baby Mammoth found in 2009 was nicknamed "Khroma" after the Khroma river in northeast Siberia.

Can the woolly mammoth be brought back?

Maybe. Because many mammoth corpses are so well preserved, scientist have been able to extract DNA from the animals. In theory, this DNA could be used to clone woolly mammoths, bringing them back from extinction. Scientists have used a gene-editing technique to insert mammoth genes into the DNA of elephant skin cells. This is far from cloning mammoths, but it is a first step to manipulating the DNA found in mammoth corpses.

About the Authors

Sanjeeb Patel

As a Software Engineer by profession, Sanjeeb recently joined Sabre Corporation as Director Software Engineering after spending more than 13 years at Walmart in the San Francisco Bay area and then in Bangalore. With a love for nature, one of his hobbies is plantation and he would like to grow thousands of trees and help make the earth a bit greener. Sanjeeb also loves to spend time helping the underprivileged wherever he can, especially in the field of education.

Sasmita Patel

With a Master's degree in computer science from California State University East Bay, Sasmita was working as a Software Engineer and then as an Online Site Merchandiser for Walmart in San Bruno, California. She later started her own business in India.

Despite coming from the corporate world, both Sanjeeb and Sasmita love to spend time working together on something different, outside and unrelated, to the corporate world. Both have recently found a new love for escaping into the wonderful world of children's books. They spend their free time discussing and writing children's stories together which often include a moral. Be sure to look for additional books in the *Animal Wisdom* series coming soon.

Their children, Simon and Sarin both join them for brainstorming when their school homework is complete. Sarin published his own book at the age of 9 called *Ultra Sarin* and Simon is currently writing his first novel that will soon to be published.

We can be reached at sanjeebpatel@gmail.com or sasmita.patel@gmail.com

We hope you enjoyed our story and would appreciate it
if you could leave us a review on Amazon.

www.ingramcontent.com/pod-product-compliance
Lightning Source LLC
Chambersburg PA
CBHW040204240726
48664CB00002B/822